PASSPORT TO SUCCESS

LAND LAW

Old Bailey Press

OLD BAILEY PRESS LTD
200 Greyhound Road, London W14 9RY

First published 1997

ISBN 1 85836 205 9

British Library Cataloguing-in-Publication.

A CIP Catalogue record for this book is available
from the British Library.

Contents

Key to journal abbreviations:

CLJ	Cambridge Law Journal
Crim LR	Criminal Law Review
CLP	Current Legal Problems
ELR	European Law Review
FLJ	Family Law Journal
LQR	Law Quarterly Review
LS	Legal Studies
LTeach	Law Teacher Journal
MLR	Modern Law Review
NLJ	New Law Journal
PL	Public Law

TOPIC 1:   Registration of Incumbrances

Land Charges (Land Charges Act 1925)

Registration of a registrable interest is deemed to constitute actual notice of that interest to all persons for all purposes connected with the land. This means that a registered charge is binding on a purchaser whether he knew about it or not, and an unregistered charged is not binding on a purchaser even if he had notice of it.

1. Registrable interests

Failure to register makes the interest void against a purchaser. Registrable land charges are divided into five classes:

a) Class A – charges imposed by statute which only arise on application by some interested person (unimportant);

b) Class B – charges imposed automatically by statute (unimportant);

c) Class C – this class is divided into four categories:

- C(i) – a puisne mortgage, ie a legal mortgage of the legal estate not protected by deposit of title deeds;

- C(ii) – a limited owner's charge. This charge is given to a tenant for life who himself pays any inheritance tax and entitles him to the same rights as a mortgagee against the settled land;

- C(iii) – a general equitable charge. This is a residuary class, and covers things such as equitable mortgages of a legal estate unprotected by deposit of title deeds and an unpaid vendor's lien;

- C(iv) – an estate contract, in other words a contract by the owner of a legal estate to convey or create a legal estate which is binding and enforceable, eg contracts for the sale, lease or mortgage of land, equitable leases arising from a purported lease lacking in the necessary formalities, options to purchase and a right of pre-emption.

d) Class D – this class is divided into three categories:

- D(i) – a charge for unpaid inheritance tax in favour of the Inland Revenue

- D(ii) – restrictive covenants made after 1925, not being covenants in a lease

- D(iii) – equitable easements arising or created after 1925, effectively confined to rights equivalent to easements and profits

e) Class E – annuities created before 1926 but registered after 1925

f) Class F – charge arising from s1 Matrimonial Homes Act 1983: the right of a spouse who does not own a legal estate in the matrimonial home to occupy it

Key cases

- *Midland Bank & Trust Co v Green* [1981] AC 513

- *Lloyds Bank v Carrick* [1996] 4 All ER 630 (CA)

Statutes

- Law of Property Act 1925, s198

- Land Charges Act 1972, s4

2. Non-registrable/overreachable interests

Examples are interests arising under a trust or settlement. If the purchase money for the land is paid to at least two trustees of the settlement (unless a trust corporation is a trustee, when the money may be paid to it) the purchaser takes free of equitable interests under the settlement, which are said to be 'overreached'. The beneficiaries' interests are transferred to the purchase money.

Key cases

- *Caunce v Caunce* [1969] 1 WLR 286

- *Hunt v Luck* [1902] 1 Ch 428

- *Kingsnorth Finance v Tizard* [1986] 1 WLR 783

Statute

- Law of Property Act 1925, s2

3. Non-registrable/non-overreachable interests

Certain interests do not come within the provision of the Land Charges Act (LCA) 1972, but do not arise under a trust or settlement, and so are not overreachable. Some of these are clearly unregistrable because of the wording of s2 LCA 1972, eg restrictive covenants and equitable easements created before 1926. Others have been declared by the courts to be unregistrable, eg:

- Beneficial interests under bare trusts
- Equitable rights of entry
- Beneficial interests under resulting trusts
- Contractual licences
- Equitable rights based on estoppel
- A charging order on an undivided share of land is now possible under the Charging Orders Act 1979, it is not registrable under LCA 1972.

The doctrine of notice applies to unregistrable interests.

Key cases

- *Ives* v *High* [1967] 2 QB 379
- *Shiloh Spinners* v *Harding* [1973] AC 691

Statute

- Land Charges Act 1925, Class D(ii) charge

Sample Questions

See questions at end of Topic 5.

Further Reading

- HLT Textbook Chapter 6
- Cheshire and Burn *Modern Law of Real Property* 15th edn 1994, Chapter 22, p713

TOPIC 2:   Registration of Title

Registration of Title (Land Registration Act 1925)

1. Types of title

a) Freehold titles

- Absolute title – where the registrar is satisfied that an applicant has shown a good title to the land, he will be registered as having an absolute title. This vests the fee simple in possession in the first registered proprietor subject only to entries on the register, overriding interests, and minor interests of which he has notice where the interests are held by beneficiaries under a trust of which he is a trustee.

- Qualified title – has same effect as an absolute title except that the proprietor holds subject to an interest specified on the register, or to interests arising prior to a specified date. Qualified title is registered where the estate owner cannot produce all the documents necessary to provide a good root of title.

- Possessory title – is subject to all estates rights and interests adverse to the first registered proprietor and subsisting at the date of first registration, even if not shown on the register. Possessory title is registered where the applicant claims title through adverse possession or where he cannot produce any documents of title apart from the conveyance to himself.

b) Leasehold titles

Generally, any leasehold interest in land for a term of years absolute where more than 21 years remain unexpired may be registered.

- Absolute leasehold title – has the same effect as an absolute freehold title, and also guarantees that the lessor has power to grant the lease and that the lease was properly granted. The lessee takes subject to the interests binding an absolute freehold owner and all the covenants and obligations of the lease.

4

- Qualified leasehold title – has the same effect as a qualified freehold title.

- Possessory leasehold title – may be granted to a lessee in possession.

- Good leasehold title – where a lessee is unable to produce documentary evidence of his landlord's title to the land, and the freehold is not registered, he can only acquire a good leasehold title. This does not guarantee that the lease was properly granted.

2. Minor interests

a) The general rule is that only minor interests protected on the register will bind a purchaser. All interests which are neither registered dispositions or overriding interests are minor interests and must be protected by registration.

Registered dispositions consist of:

- Fee simple absolute in possession
- Legal leases exceeding 21 years
- Legal rentcharges
- Legal easements
- Legal mortgages

Overriding interests are considered below (see (3)).

b) There are two classes of minor interest:

- Interests capable of being overreached on a proper sale, ie the interests of the beneficiaries under a trust for sale or a strict settlement.

- Interests which will not bind a purchaser unless registered. These include:

  – Equitable interests registrable under the LCA 1972 for unregistered land

  – Miscellaneous equitable interests which are not registrable under LCA 1972, eg interests under bare trusts, beneficial interests under resulting trusts

Legal interests arising under a lease for 21 years or less, granted rent-free or at a fine.

c) There are four methods of protecting minor interests, effective from the date of registration.

- Notice (s52(1) LRA 1925) – this is entered in the charges register, and ensures that any future dealings with the land take place subject to the interest protected by the notice. It can only be entered if the land certificate is produced, and so generally can only be done if the registered proprietor agrees.

- Caution (ss53–56 LRA 1925) – merely gives the person entering it a right to be warned of any impending transaction with the land and gives him time to object. It is used when a notice cannot be entered because the land certificate cannot be obtained, and is weaker protection than a registered land charge in unregistered land because:

  - It puts the onus on the cautioner to take steps to protect his interests.

  - It can be 'warned off' at any time by the registered proprietor requiring notice to be given to the cautioner that he must defend his claim within a given time.

  - It does not confer priority on the cautioned interest over a subsequently registered charge.

- Inhibitions (s57 LRA 1925) – an order of the court or the registrar forbidding all dealings with the land either for a specified time period or until a specified event or until further notice. Though usually a last resort, it is used routinely when the registered proprietor becomes bankrupt.

- Restrictions (s58(1) LRA 1925) – prevents dealing with the land until some condition is complied with, but unlike an inhibition it is not hostile to the registered proprietor. It is used, for example, when land is held on trust for sale or is settled land, to ensure that the overreaching mechanism is gone through.

Key cases

- *Mortgage Corporation* v *Nationwide Credit Corporation* [1993] 4 All ER 623

- *William & Glyn's Bank* v *Boland* [1981] AC 487

Statutes

- Land Registration Act (LRA) 1925, s20 and s59(6)

- Law of Property Act (LPA) 1925, s2

3. Overriding interests

a) Defined in s3(xvi) LRA 1925 as:

'all the incumbrances, interests and powers not entered on the register, but subject to which registered disposition are to take effect'.

These are, therefore, rights which bind a purchaser without appearing on the register, even though he has no knowledge of them.

b) There are two classes of overriding interest:

- Minor interests which are not protected by registration but are protected under s70(1)(g) and converted into overriding interests.

- Those specifically listed in s70(1) LRA 1925, although often in broad and uncertain terms. The most important of these are s70(1)(a), (f), (g) and (k):

  - Section 70(1)(a) is obviously intended to protect legal easements and profits à prendre created (1) before the servient tenement was registered, and (2) other than by express grant or reservation, and also equitable profits à prendre. However, the meaning of the words 'equitable easements required to be protected by notice' is unclear.

The general opinion of textbook writers and the Land Registry is that equitable easements cannot be overriding interests but in *Celsteel Ltd* v *Alton House Holdings Ltd* [1985] 1 WLR 204 it was held that an equitable easement was a 'right enjoyed with the land' for the purpose of that rule. As it affected the registered title it was an 'overriding interest' which did not need to be protected by notice on the register.

- Section 70(1)(f) provides for the rights arising by adverse possession (see s75 LRA 1925).

- Section 70(1)(k) is intended to protect those leases which cannot be registered dispositions because they were granted for 21 years or less.

  Leases for 21 years or less which do not qualify under s70(1)(k) are registerable as minor interests, or may come within s70(1)(g) as 'rights' protected by 'actual occupation'.

- Before s70(1)(g) can apply three conditions must be satisfied:

  1. There must be a right 'subsisting in relation to the land' which is capable of being protected by s70(1)(g): *Williams & Glyn's Bank* v *Boland* [1981] AC 487.

     Rights which can only be minor interests, and hence cannot be protected by s70(1)(g), are those: of a beneficiary under a Settled Land Act settlement; of a tenant arising from a notice under the Leasehold Reform Act 1967 of his desire to have the freehold or an extended lease; and of occupation of a spouse under Matrimonial Homes Act 1983.

  2. The owner of the right must be in actual occupation of the land or in receipt of the rents or profits therefrom affected by the right.

     The date when the owner must be in occupation is the date of the mortgage, which will exclude from the protection of s70(1)(g) many purchasers who do not occupy until after the mortgage is completed (which is usual in the case of many purchases of residential premises): see further *Abbey National Building Society* v *Cann* [1990] 2

WLR 832 and *Lloyd's Bank plc* v *Rosset* [1990] 2 WLR 867 HL.

3. The saving clause to s70(1)(g) requires that the purchaser must have made inquiry of the owner of the right, and not been told of the right. Inquiry of the vendor alone will suffice, it must be the person in 'actual occupation'.

If the three requirements are satisfied, the right claimed is converted by actual occupation from a minor interest into an overriding interest – which, of course, need not be protected by registration.

Key cases

- *Abbey National Building Society* v *Cann*, above

- *Bridges* v *Mees* [1957] Ch 475

- *Celsteel* v *Alton House Holdings*, above

- *City of London Building Society* v *Flegg* [1987] 2 WLR 1266

- *Lloyd's Bank* v *Rossett*, above

- *Williams & Glyn's Bank* v *Boland*, above

- *Skipton Building Society* v *Clayton* (1993) The Times 25 March

- *Woolwich Building Society* v *Dickman* [1996] 3 All ER 204 (CA)

Statutes

- Land Registration Act 1925, s70(1)(a), (f), (g) and (k)

- Law of Property Act 1925, s2

```
                              Registered Title
                                    │
        ┌───────────────────────────┼───────────────────────────┐
  Registered interests         Minor interests          Overriding interests not on
  (property register)                                    register (s70(1) LRA 1925)
                                    │
                    ┌───────────────┴───────────────┐
          Protected proprietorship              Not so protected
          or charges register
                    │
        ┌───────────┬───────────────┬───────────────┐
    Notice       Caution        Inhibition       Restriction
   (s52(1) LRA   (ss53–56      (s57 LRA 1925)   (s58(1) LRA 1925)
    1925)         LRA 1925)
```

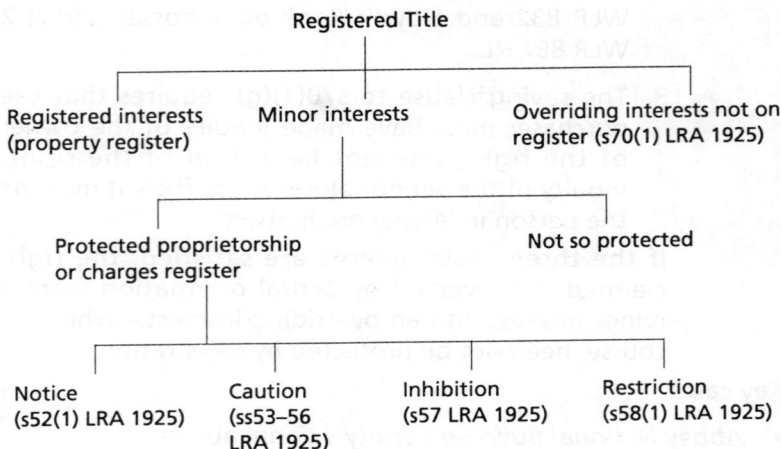

Sample Questions

See Questions at end of Topic 5.

Further Reading

- HLT Textbook Chapter 7
- Gray *Elements of Land Law* 2nd edn 1993, Chapters 6 and 8
- Dixon 'Acquiring an Interest in Another's Property: *Lloyd's Bank* v *Rosset'* [1991] CLJ 38
- Tee 'Gentlly Reforming Land Registration: The Latest Law Commission Report and Draft Bill' [1996] CLJ 241

TOPIC 3:   Settled Land

Strict Settlements

1. Definition

A settlement is created by any document or documents which deal with land in one of the ways set out in s1(1) of the Settled Land Act (SLA) 1925, eg:

- Where the land stands for the time being limited in trust for any persons by way of succession. The most common example of such a limitation is 'to A for life and then to B in fee simple'.

- Entails, eg 'to A for an entailed interest'

- An estate subject to a gift over on the failure of issue or other event

- A determinable fee

- Where land is given to an infant

- Where the land is subject to a family rentcharge, eg 'to A in fee simple but charged with the payment of £1,000 per annum to A's widow during her lifetime'.

2. Creation

a) By s4(1) SLA 1925 every settlement must be effected by two documents, a trust instrument and a vesting deed. The latter contains all that a purchaser of the settled land needs to know, while the details of the trust are contained in the trust instrument which the purchaser is not entitled to see. These details are said to be 'behind the veil' or to be subject to the 'curtain principle'. The object is to enable the land to be sold easily in spite of the beneficial interests of the settlement.

b) The vesting deed must:

- Describe the settled land

- Declare that the settled land is vested in the person

named as tenant for life on the trusts contained in the trust instrument

- Contain the names of the trustees of the settlement
- Contain any additional powers of the tenant for life
- Name the persons with power to appoint new trustees

The vesting deed vests the legal fee simple in the person who for the time being is to have the enjoyment of the land itself. The tenant for life obtains the legal estate which is held on the trusts of the settlement.

c) The trust instrument must:

- Declare the trusts affecting the settled land
- Appoint or constitute trustees of the settlement
- Contain the power, if any, to appoint new trustees of the settlement
- Set out any additional powers
- Bear any stamp duty payable

If an inter vivos settlement is not made by means of a vesting deed and a trust instrument, then by s4(1) the legal estate is not transferred and therefore remains in the settlor. The only way this can be put right is by the trustees executing a vesting deed (s9(2)).

3. **Holder of legal estate/tenant for life**

a) Section 19 contains the general definition of a tenant for life which applies to most settlements:

'The person of full age who is for the time being beneficially entitled under a settlement to possession of the settled land for his life is for the purposes of this Act the tenant for life of that land ...'

b) However, because of the wide definition of settled land in s1(1) SLA 1925, it is necessary to define 'tenant for life' in special cases with more particularity. Section 20 provides that each of the following persons (when of full age in possession) have the powers of a tenant for life:

- A tenant in tail

- A person with a conditional fee

- A person entitled to a base or determinable fee

- A tenant for years determinable on life, not holding merely under a lease at a rent. This definition excludes a person paying even a nominal rent.

- A person entitled to the income of land under a trust during his own or any other life.

- A person entitled in fee simple subject to family charges.

If the land is subject to an immediate binding trust for sale, the person so entitled is not a tenant for life and the land is not settled land.

c) When there is no tenant for life, then by s23 those powers are vested in the statutory owner, defined in s117(1)(xxvi) as either:

- The person of full age on whom the settlement expressly conveys the powers of a tenant for life; or

- (more commonly) the trustees of the settlement.

Key Case

- *Dent* v *Dent* [1996] 1 WLR 683; [1996] 1 All ER 659 (Ch D)

4. Powers of tentant for life (Sale, Mortgage, Lease)

The various powers of the tenant for life are demonstrated by the following diagram:

Powers exercisable on giving notice to the trustees	Powers exercisable (A) With the consent of the trustees	Powers exercisable without either notice to or consent of the trustees or the court
1. Sale, ss38–39 2. Lease, ss41–48 3. Exchange, ss38–40 4. Grant Options, s51 (all the above require *general notice* which states the intention to exercise a power but without being specific) 5. Mortgage, s71 (following the giving of *specific notice*)	1. Compromise or settle disputes, s58(1) 2. Release rights imposed on other land for benefit of settled land, s58(2)	1. Make improvements, ss83–89 2. Accept surrenders of leases, s52 3. To take leases of other lands, s53 4. To make leases of less than 21 years, s42(5)
	(B) *With the consent of the trustees or the court*	
	1. To cut and sell timber, s66 2. To dispose of the principal mansion house, s65(1)	
	(C) *With the consent of the court*	
	1. To sell heirlooms, s67 2. To effect any transaction not otherwise authorised by the Act or settlement if it is for the benefit of the land or beneficiaries, s64 3. To grant building/ mining leases for terms longer than in the Act, s46	

Key cases

- *Re Acklom* [1929] 1 Ch 195

- *Wheelwright* v *Walker* (1883) 23 Ch D 752

5. Trustees of the settlement

a) Section 30 SLA 1925 sets out five definitions, each of which must be applied in turn; if there is no person within head (1) then head (2) must be examined, but if there are persons within head (1) then they will be trustees of the settlement and there is no need to look at head (2). The various heads are:

- The persons who under the settlement are trustees with power to sell or to consent to or to approve sale.

- The persons expressly declared by the settlement to be 'trustees for the purposes of the Settled Land Act'.

- Persons who under the settlement are trustees with power to sell other land comprised in the settlement.

- Persons who under the settlement are trustees with future powers to sell or under a future trust for sale.

- Persons appointed by deed by those able to dispose of the whole equitable interest in the settled land.

b) When a settlement arises under a will or intestacy, and there are no trustees under any other provisions, the personal representatives are trustees until others are appointed (s30(3)).

c) Where none of the above provisions apply, or it is expedient, an application can be made to the court under s34 by the tenant for life, statutory owner or other person interested for appointment of trustees.

Sample Questions

See Questions at the end of Topic 5.

Further Reading

- HLT Textbook Chapter 8
- Gray Chapter 15

See further Topic 12: Reform: The New Law on Trusts of Land.

TOPIC 4:   Trusts for Sale

1. Definition and types

a) A trust for sale is an *immediate binding* trust for sale. There must be a duty to sell and not just a mere power to sell, though there may exist a right to postpone sale.

- The trust itself must be effective immediately, although the duty to sell can be postponed.

- To be binding the trust for sale must embrace the whole legal estate which is the subject matter of the settlement.

A trust for sale is excluded from the provisions of the SLA 1925 and the powers of dealing with the land are vested in the trustees.

b) Types of trust for sale include:

- express trusts, ie those arising expressly from the wording of the settlement; and

- statutory trusts, eg when two or more persons are jointly entitled to land: see Topic 5.

Statutes

- Law of Property Act 1925, s205, ss34–36

2. To sell or not?

a) Unless a contrary intention appears, a power to postpone sale is implied in every trust for sale by s25 LPA 1925. However, because there is a trust for sale, there is a duty to sell, and any trustee can compel his co-trustees to do their duty but they must be unanimous if they wish to exercise a power. Therefore the land must be sold unless all trustees agree to postpone. However, the court will not enforce a sale if that would defeat the object of the trust or if it would be in breach of a contractual obligation on the trustees.

The rule is particularly relevant as regards the family home, where the court may conclude that a secondary purpose of the trust was to acquire the property as a family home. If that purpose still exists (at the time of the application) the court will not usually grant an order for sale.

b) Trusts for sale may be made subject to a condition that the land shall not be sold without the consent of the named person or persons (s28(1)). Trustees who fail to obtain such consent will be in breach of trust, but a purchaser for value need only ensure that the consent of two such persons is obtained to be protected: s26(1) LPA 1925. Thus the powers of the trustees may be effectively curtailed.

Key cases

- *Re Inns* [1947] Ch 576

- *Re Mayo* [1943] 2 All ER 440; [1943] Ch 302

3. Overreaching or conversion

Theoretically there is no overreaching in a trust for sale because of the doctrine of conversion means that from the very creation of the trust the beneficiary's rights are rights in money not in land. However, as with settlements the purchase money must be paid to at least two trustees or a trust corporation in order for the purchaser to take free of the rights of the beneficiaries.

Key cases

- *Irani Finance* v *Singh* [1971] Ch 59

- *Williams & Glyn's Bank* v *Boland* [1981] AC 487

Statutes

- Law of Property Act 1925, s2 and s205

Summary – Comparison of the Strict Settlement and the Trust for Sale

Feature	Strict settlement	Trust for sale
1. Controlling Act	Settled Land Act 1925	Law of Property Act 1925
2. Legal Estate	Vested in tenant for life or statutory owners, s19(1)	Vested in trustees for sale, s28(1)
3. Documents	Two documents must be used – the vesting deed and the trust instrument, s4(1)	Only one document required but two are often used to keep the trusts off the title
4. Sale	Tenant for life has a power to sell, s38	Trustees for sale under a duty to sell, s205(1)(xxix)
5. Conversion	No application to a strict settlement	Converts land held on trust for sale into personalty
6. Restrictions on powers	Settlor cannot restrict the powers of the tenant for life, s106	Settlor can place restrictions by way of consents and there is a power to postpone sale, s25, s26(1), and *Re Inns* (1947)
7. Application of capital money	Decided by the tenant for life on the basis of the settlement, s73 and s75(2)	Decided by the trustees for sale, s28(1)

Sample Questions

See Questions at end of Topic 5.

Further Reading

- HLT Textbook Chapters 5 and 8
- Gray Chapters 11 and 12

See further Topic 12: Reform: The New Law on Trusts of Land.

TOPIC 5: Co-ownership

1. Types: joint tenancy or tenancy in common

Where land is held by co-owners, during their lifetimes each is entitled to live on or share in the proceeds of the land. But on the death of a co-owner the way in which his interest in the land devolves, depends on the type of co-ownership. Assuming A and B made an equal contribution to the purchase price of a property:

Joint tenancy	*Tenancy in common*
A–B	A–B
A dies leaving two children C and D	A dies leaving two children C and D
The result is:	The result is:
B takes all as survivor ('right of survivorship')	B – C – D 1/2 1/4 1/4 They hold as tenants in common

Since the 1925 property legislation came into effect only a joint tenancy can exist at law. A tenancy in common must be held behind a trust.

2. Acquisition of a beneficial interest

a) Resulting trusts

Under a resulting trust the person(s) in whom the legal estate is vested must hold the equitable interest on trust for all those entitled to it as equitable co-owners. A resulting trust may arise in the following ways.

- Express trust in conveyance
- Financial contributions/repairs and improvements

  Key cases

  - *Burns* v *Burns* [1984] 1 All ER 244
  - *Gissing* v *Gissing* [1971] AC 886
  - *Pettitt* v *Pettitt* [1970] AC 777

19

b) Constructive trusts

A constructive trust has similar consequences as those of a resulting trust (above) and may arise in the following ways:

- Express informal agreement

  Key cases

  - *Lloyd's Bank* v *Rossett* [1990] 2 WLR 867

  - *Springette* v *Defoe* (1992) The Independent 24 March; [1992] 2 FLR 388

- Direct financial contribution

  Key case

  - *Lloyd's Bank* v *Rossett*, above

  - *Drake* v *Whipp* (1995) The Times 19 December (CA)

  - *Midland Bank plc* v *Cooke* [1995] 4 All ER 562 (CA)

c) Proprietary estoppel

- General

  The principal of proprietary estoppel may sometimes be relied on in circumstances similar to those which may give rise to a resulting or constructice trust, with similar consequences.

  Key case

  - *Taylors Fashions* v *Liverpool Victoria Trustees* [1981] 1 All ER 897

- Representation

  Key cases

  - *Re Basham* [1986] 1 WLR 1498

  - *Grant* v *Edwards* [1986] Ch 638

- Reliance

  Key cases

  - *Grant* v *Edwards*, above

  - *Jones* v *Jones* [1977] 1 WLR 438

d) Protection of beneficiary

Whenever there is beneficial co-ownership in possession of land (other than settled land) the legal estate must be held on a trust for sale. If the conveyence does not expressly provide for a trust, a statutory trust is imposed and the courts have made use of s36(4) SLA 1925 to rectify the lack of any expression of trust, so as to protect the beneficial ownership.

Key cases

- *Bull* v *Bull* [1955] 1 QB 234

- *Jones* v *Challenger* [1961] 1 QB 176

- *Re Buchanan-Wollastan's Conveyance* [1939] Ch 738

Statutes

- Law of Property Act 1925, s26, s30

- Settled Land Act 1925, s36(4)

d) Severance

A joint tenant who wishes his interest to pass to a person other than the remaining joint tenants cannot give effect to his wishes by will, as the right of survivorship comes into operation on his death. However, he can avoid the right of survivorship by converting his joint tenancy into a tenancy in common during his lifetime. This process is called severance and can be effected by:

- Alienation inter vivos by a joint tenant

- Mutual agreement among joint tenants

- The provisions of s36(2) LPA 1925, ie by the joint tenant giving written notice to the other joint tenants

- Homicide

- Acquisition of another estate in land, because this destroys the unity of interest

- Bankruptcy

- A course of dealing in which one party makes clear to the other(s) that he desires that their shares should no longer be held jointly but in common, or in which both or all parties evince such an intention.

Key cases

- *Burgess* v *Rawnsley* [1975] Ch 429
- *Re Draper's Conveyance* [1969] 1 Ch 486
- *Re Dennis (A Bankrupt)* [1995] 3 All ER 171
- *Re Palmer (Deceased) (A Debtor)* [1994] 3 All ER 835

Statute

- Law of Property Act 1925, s36(2)

Sample Questions

See below.

Further Reading

- HLT Textbook Chapter 9
- Cheshire and Burn Chapter 10, p207
- Ferguson 'Estate Contracts, Constructive Trusts and the Land Charges Act' (1996) 112 LQR 549
- Gardner 'A Woman's Work: *Lloyd's Bank* v *Rosset*'(1991) 54 MLR 126
- Lunney 'Never Trust a Man' (1993) 56 MLR 87
- Milne 'Proprietary Estoppel in a Procrustean Bed' (1995) 58 MLR 412
- Nolan 'The Triumph of Technicality' [1996] CLJ 436
- O'Hagan 'Indirect Contributions to the Purchase of Property' (1993) 56 MLR 224
- Oldham 'Quantification of Beneficial Interest in Land' [1996] CLJ 194

Sample Questions for Topics 1–5

1. a) The title to 'The Elms' is unregistered. How would you expect the following interests to be protected against subsequent purchasers?

i) A legal mortgage of The Elms with the Upshire Building Society who obtained the title deeds as security.

ii) An option to purchase The Elms granted in 1980.

iii) A restrictive covenant not to build more than one residential house on the land forming the site of The Elms. This covenant was made at the time The Elms was built in 1890.

iv) The son of the present owner planted a new orchard in the grounds of The Elms on the strength of a verbal promise given by his father that 'The Elms will be yours one day'.

v) The right of the wife of the present owner to remain in occupation of The Elms following the departure of her husband in 1991. He has never returned.

and

b) How would your answers to the above question a) i-v differ if the title to The Elms had been registered in 1960 with Absolute title?

2. 'A purchaser of land must satisfy himself on two separate matters; firstly, that the vendor is entitled to convey the land, and, secondly, that there are no encumbrances in favour of third parties which will continue to bind the land after the conveyance'.

To what extent do the Land Registration Act 1925 and the Land Charges Act 1972 assist the purchaser in this context?

3. a) Explain the circumstances in which an unregistered title must be made the subject of an application for first registration at HM Land Registry.

and

b) Explain the effects of registration with qualified and possessory titles. Give examples of title defects which may lead to such titles being granted.

4. 'The lack of a residual category of land charge in the Land Charges Act 1972 is undoubtedly its greatest single defect.'

Discuss the validity of this statement.

5. In 1991 Rachel decided she wished to buy the council house in which she had lived for many years. She was entitled to a 25% discount on the value of the property because of her period of occupation.

   The purchase price was raised by Rachel and her two sons, Stephen and Thomas in equal shares of one third of the purchase price each. The house was conveyed into Rachel's sole name. When she died, her will disclosed that she had left the property to her sister Rebecca. Rebecca wants to go and live in the house but Stephen and Thomas want the house sold and are claiming one third each of the sale price.

   Advise Rebecca.

6. 'Equity leans against joint tenants and favours tenancies in common'. Explain the meaning of this maxim and show how the Courts have applied the principle.

   Can the continuing application of this principle be justified today?

7. In 1980 John suggested to Mary, his mother, who was old and in poor health, that they should buy a house together. Mary agreed and, knowing that John had little money, offered to pay £50,000 towards the purchase price. The house, which was unregistered land, was conveyed into John's sole name. The purchase price of the house was £100,000 and the remaining £50,000 was raised by means of a building society mortgage for which John was solely responsible. Mary knew nothing of the mortgage. A few years later John obtained, again without Mary's knowledge, a loan of £70,000 from Quickloans Ltd, at a relatively high rate of interest, secured by a charge on the house in his sole name. Although Quickloans knew that Mary was living in the house, they made no inquiries of her. John used part of the £70,000 to redeem the first mortgage, pocketed the rest and disappeared. Quickloans subsequently sought possession of the house from Mary the mortgage instalments have not been paid.

   Advise Mary.

8. Jim was the registered owner of Blackacre and in 1990 he orally agreed to sell a part of the land to his friend, Ben, for £20,000. Ben did not pay anything, but he built a house on the part he had agreed to purchase and went into occupation. In

1992 Jim sold the whole of Blackacre to Victor and Victor was registered as the new owner. Victor has now told Ben to leave the land.

Advise Ben.

Would your advice be different if either (a) the agreement between Jim and Ben had been in writing, or (b) Blackacre had been sold to Victor expressly 'subject to Ben's rights'?

9. When Stella decided to buy a farm, she invited her lover, Paul, to come and live with her and help her run the farm. Stella paid the whole purchase price and the farm was conveyed into her sole name. When Paul asked why it had not been conveyed into their joint names, Stella told him that there was no need for him to worry as he would get a half-share when they got married and as she was going to leave him her London apartment in her will anyway. Stella and Paul never married but they worked hard on the farm for several years, sharing the profits equally, and as a result the value of the farm doubled. Recently Stella has died leaving all her estate to her mother. Paul now claims both the farm and the London apartment.

Advise Stella's mother.

10. 'Now that positive remedies are awarded by way of constructive trust or by the application of the doctrine of proprietary estoppel, it is clear that the licensee may have an interest which is both binding on third parties and capable of being bought and sold. In such circumstances, the conclusion cannot be avoided that in view of recent developments some licences are indeed interests in land'. (Cheshire and Burn's Modern Law of Real Property).

Discuss the validity of this analysis.

TOPIC 6: Leases

1. Definitions

- **Lease:** a contract either in writing or by deed granting a leasehold estate in land.
- **Tenancy:** the interest held under a lease. A tenancy can be granted orally, by a tenancy agreement.
- **Demise:** the grant of a tenancy.
- **Covenant:** a promise expressly made in a lease, or implied into a lease or tenancy agreement by statute or at common law.
- **Rent:** the consideration given by a tenant to his landlord in return for the grant of a tenancy. Rent is paid throughout the term. It usually takes the form of money, but need not.
- **Fine or premium:** a lump sum paid by a tenant at the beginning of the term. If a fine is paid, usually it is only very low, or no rent is payable for the remainder of the term.
- **Determination:** the coming to an end of a tenancy.
- **Reversion:** the interest in the land held by a landlord during the subsistence of a lease.

A number of words are used interchangeably for 'landlord' and 'tenant':

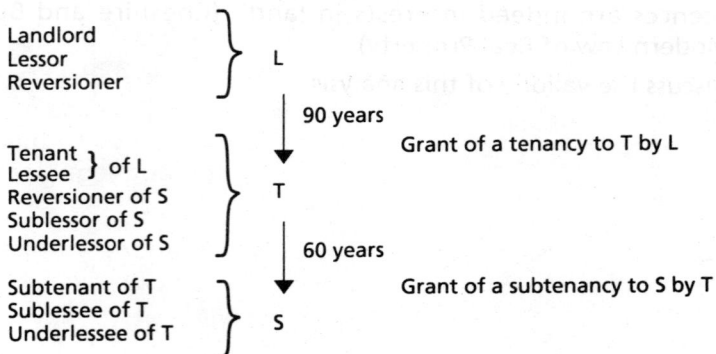

Landlord Lessor Reversioner	} L	
	↓ 90 years	Grant of a tenancy to T by L
Tenant } of L Lessee Reversioner of S Sublessor of S Underlessor of S	} T	
	↓ 60 years	Grant of a subtenancy to S by T
Subtenant of T Sublessee of T Underlessee of T	} S	

This may also be demonstrated by the following diagram:

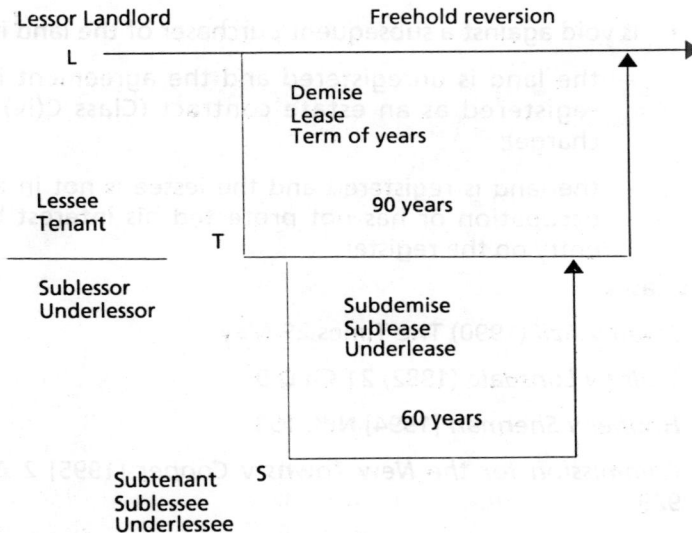

2. Formalities and equitable leases

a) In order to grant a valid legal estate, a lease must comply with three requirements:

- It must be in the correct form;

- It must be certain in duration; and

- The tenant must have exclusive possession.

As a general rule a legal lease must be made by deed.

b) A specifically enforceable lease is regarded as a valid equitable lease under the rule in *Walsh* v *Lonsdale* (1882) 21 Ch D 9, ie 'equity regards as done, that which ought to be done'. An equitable lease is as good as a legal lease for many purposes except that it:

- Depends for its validity on the discretionary remedy of specific performance, which may not be available – if the tenant is in breach of a covenant;

- Does not carry with it easements and other rights under s62 LPA 1925 because it is not a conveyance;
- Is void against a subsequent purchaser of the land if:
  - the land is unregistered and the agreement is not registered as an estate contract (Class C(iv) land charge);
  - the land is registered and the lessee is not in actual occupation or has not protected his interest by an entry on the register.

Key cases

- *Javad* v *Azil* (1990) The Times 29 May
- *Walsh* v *Lonsdale* (1882) 21 Ch D 9
- *Hooper* v *Sherman* [1994] NPC 153
- *Commission for the New Towns* v *Cooper* [1995] 2 All ER 929
- *Prudential Assurance Co* v *London Residuary Body* [1992] 3 WLR 279

Statutes

- Law of Property Act 1925, s52, s54(2)
- Law of Property (Miscellaneous Provisions) Act 1989, s2
- Land Registration Act 1925, s70(1)(g)
- Land Charges Act 1925, C(iv)

3. **Notice to quit**

Effective if given by only one joint tenant

Key case

- *Hammersmith and Fulham LBC* v *Monk* [1991] 3 WLR 1144

4. **Leasehold covenants**

a) **Implied covenants**

Obligations are implied into leases both at common law and by statute, and can be expressly excluded, but in the absence of express provision, both landlords and tenants are subject to implied covenants. There are two situations to consider:

- Position in the absence of express provision – certain covenants will be implied, eg landlord's obligations for quiet enjoyment, repairs, fitness for occupation, and tenant's obligations to pay rent, rates, taxes and to permit landlord to enter and view the premises.

- Usual covenants where the parties may have agreed to be bound by the 'usual covenants' (a species of implied term). The phrase is generally taken to refer to the following covenants:

  - By the tenant   to pay tenant's rates and taxes;

    to pay rent;

    to keep the premises in repair and deliver them up in repair;

    if the landlord has undertaken to repair, to permit the landlord to enter and view the state of repair;

    a condition for re-entry on non-payment of rent.

  - By the landlord   for quiet enjoyment.

Key case

- *Liverpool City Council v Irwin* [1977] AC 239

Statute

- Defective Premises Act 1972

b) Express covenants

A carefully drafted lease may contain a large number of express covenants, most of them by the tenant, which regulate the parties' conduct under the lease. It is always necessary to decide whether any alleged breach falls within the precise wording of the covenant.

- To pay rent

  - The covenant should stipulate the rent and the dates on which it is payable.

- If not expressly made payable in advance it is payable in arrear.

- It remains payable even though the premises are destroyed or rendered uninhabitable, unless the lease expressly stipulates otherwise.

The landlord can enforce payment of rent:

- By suing in contract for the money

- By distress

- By forfeiture

Remedies: formal demand, distress, arrears: Common Law Procedure Act 1852

- Repairs

The following principles have been established by the case law:

- If the problem is caused by an inherent defect, remedial work is not within the repairing covenant unless the defect has caused damage to the building or its contents.

- If the inherent defect causes deterioration to the building, carrying out remedial work beyond the terms of the repairing covenant is not justified.

- If remedial work is necessary within the terms of the covenant, this may extend to the remedy of the inherent defect itself.

- There is no 'disrepair' within the covenant to repair if there is no proof of physical deterioration to the building.

Normally an injunction or decree of specific performance cannot be obtained for a breach of a repairing covenant, except where the landlord is in breach and the tenant is unable to repair because the breach concerns property not demised to him.

Key cases

- *Lurcott* v *Wakely* [1911] 1 KB 505

- *Proudfoot* v *Hart* (1890) 25 QBD 42

- Remedies

 - Damages

 - Forfeiture

 Statutes

 - Leasehold Property (Repairs) Act 1938, s1

 - Landlord and Tenant Act 1927, s18

- Assigning etc

 Construction

 It is a question of construction as to whether there is an absolute or qualified covenant not to assign, underlet or part with possession of the demised premises.

 With an absolute covenant, the tenant may not assign etc the demised premises. The landlord may, however, waive the covenant.

 With a qualified covenant not to assign etc without the landlord's consent, by s19(1) Landlord and Tenant Act 1927 such consent is not to be unreasonably withheld. If the landlord gives reasons for refusal the burden of proving unreasonableness is on the tenant, otherwise it is on the landlord.

 Statutes

 - Landlord and Tenant Act 1927, s19

 - Landlord and Tenant (Covenants) Act, 1995

 Reasonableness

 Key cases

 - *International Drilling Fluids* v *Louisville Investments* [1986] 2 WLR 581

 Remedies

 - Forfeiture

Statutes

– Law of Property Act 1925, s146

Assignment of the reversion

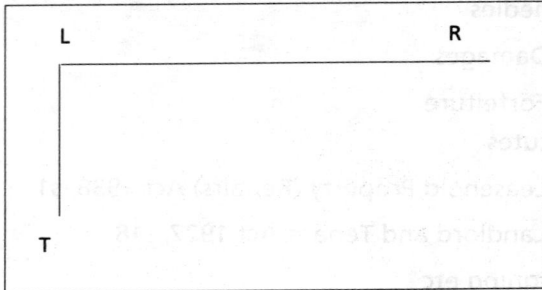

```
L                              R
 ┌─────────────────────────────
 │
 │
 │
 │
 T
```

Assignment of the lease

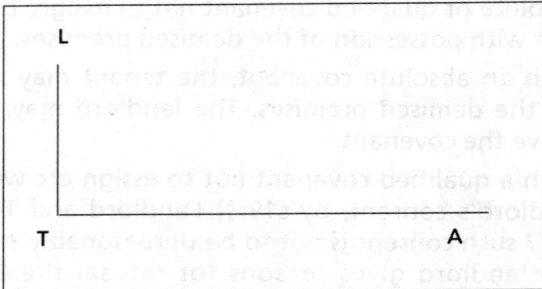

```
        L                      R
         ┌─────────────────────
         │
         │
         T                     A
```

Subtenancy

```
 L's fee simple

    L  ┌─ ─ ─ ─ ─ ─ ─ ─ ┐ L
 Grant to T  │                │ 2060
 of 90-year  │1970            │
 lease       │      90 years  │ Reversion
    ▼                 ▲         to L
    T        T        │
             ┌─ ─ ─ ─ ─ ┐ 2030
 Grant to S  │          │
 of 40-year  │1990      │ Reversion
 lease       │ 40 years │ to T
    S        ▼
```

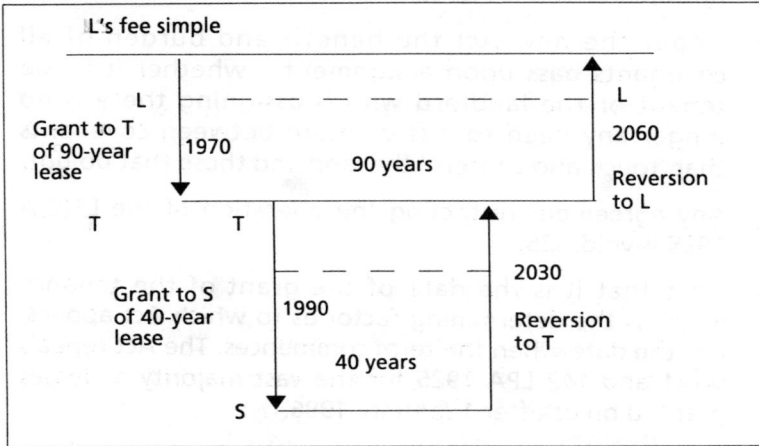

5. Enforceability of covenants

a) Covenants in leases granted before 1 January 1996 are enforceable between parties where there is privity of contract or privity of estate.

   Note how the doctrine of privity applies to sub-tenants, eg *Tulk v Moxhay* (1848) 2 Ph 774: see further Topic 8, Restrictive Covenants.

   Statutes

   - Law of Property Act 1925, ss141, 142 and 146(2).

b) For tenancies granted after 31 December 1995 the position is governed by the Landlord and Tenant (Covenants) Act 1995.

   Key points of LT(C)A 1995:

   - It makes provision for persons bound by covenants of a tenancy to be released from them on the assignment of the tenancy.

   - It applies to all covenants in a tenancy apart from certain covenants arising under the Housing Act 1985 (for repayment of discount on early disposals).

- The LT(C)A 1995 differentiates between new tenancies (granted after the Act came into force) and others.

- Under the new Act the benefit and burden of all covenants pass upon assignment – whether it is the tenant or the landlord who is assigning there is no longer any need to differentiate between covenants that 'touch and concern' the land and those that do not.

- Any agreement restricting the operation of the LT(C)A 1995 is void: s25.

- Note that it is the date of the grant of the tenancy which is the determining factor as to which Act applies, not the date when the term commences. The Act repeals ss141 and 142 LPA 1925 for the vast majority of leases granted on or after 1 January 1996.

- The content of the assignment clause in new tenancies is likely to be a key area in leasehold negotiations, since landlords can now specify the security/creditworthiness criteria that a prospective assignee will have to meet. The Act may result in an increased use of subletting to avoid the consequences of tenant release, as it does not apply to subletting.

6. Forfeiture

a) A landlord can forfeit a tenancy at any time where the tenant is in breach of covenant, so long as the right to forfeit (or re-enter) is reserved in the lease. Every lease should contain such a right (known as a 'proviso for re-entry') as a matter of course.

b) Forfeiture is normally used to determine terms certain, where the term still has some time to run. Periodic tenancies can be forfeit, but the procedure would be appropriate only for longer periodic tenancies.

c) Before a landlord can forfeit a lease he must:

- Establish that he has the right to forfeit the lease by ensuring the lease contains the necessary forfeiture clause.

- Ensure that there is no waiver of that right.

- Comply with s146 LPA 1925 (for all breaches except breach of a covenant to pay rent), ie serve statutory notice on the tenant and give tenant reasonable time to comply.

- Bring possession proceedings in court.

d) A s146 notice need not be served in the following cases:

- breach of covenant to pay rent;

- breach of covenant to allow inspection in mining leases;

- bankruptcy of the tenant in cetain specific types of lease, including those of agricultural land and public houses (see s146(9) LPA 1925).

e) A lease is not forfeited until the proceedings are served on the tenant. Once the lease has been declared forfeited by a court, the tenant and any subtenants may apply for relief from forfeiture. Section 146(2) LPA 1925 gives the court a wide discretion to allow the tenant relief from forfeiture, on terms that the breach ceases, but does not apply where the landlord has already re-entered. The court will not allow relief where:

- The breach is irremediable

- The landlord has already re-entered

In regard to forfeiture for non-payment of rent where the landlord brings an action for possession the tenant has the right under s212 Common Law Procedure Act 1852 to have the action discontinued if he pays all arrears and costs at any time before the trial. However, it was held in *Standard Pattern Co Ltd v Ivey* [1962] Ch 432 that this section is confined to cases where at least half a year's rent is due.

f) Even after judgment has been given the court can give the tenant relief from forfeiture ss210–212 Common Law Procedure Act 1852.

- The tenant must apply within six months of the judgment (but the limit does not apply if the landlord re-entered other than by action for possession).

- Relief will be granted if he pays the rent due and the landlord's costs, and if it is equitable in the circumstances.
- Relief may be granted on terms, eg that the tenant should do outstanding repairs.

Key cases

- *Rugby School* v *Tannahill* [1935] 1 KB 87
- *Scala House and District Properties* v *Forbes* [1974] QB 575

Where the tenant has assigned his interest

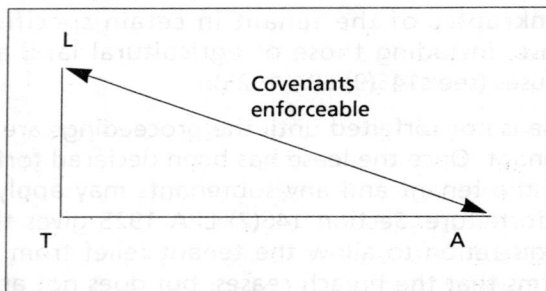

Enforcement by and against subtenants

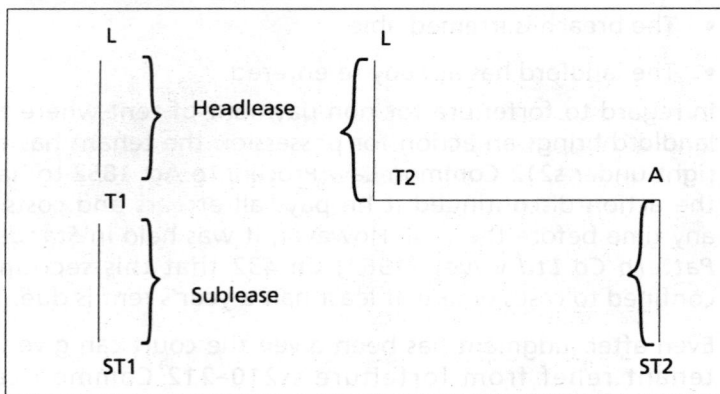

Sample Questions

1. In 1989 Leslie granted Alice a lease of Redstone House (unregistered land) for 20 years, Alice covenanting, inter alia, to pay a yearly rent of £10,000 to keep the house in a good state of repair and not to use the house for immoral purposes. In 1990 Alice assigned her lease to Bert and in 1993 Bert granted a sublease to Chris for five years. In 1993 Leslie assigned his reversion to Rachel. No rent has been paid since 1991, the house is in serious need of repair and Chris has recently been convicted of keeping a brothel.

   Who has remedies against whom in respect of these breaches of covenant?

2. Consider the effect of

   a) a lease of Redacre at a rent to Alf until he marries;

   b) a lease of Pinkacre at a rent to Bill for five years which contains a covenant to renew on the same terms;

   c) a lease of Greenacre at a yearly rent to Cal until the landlord requires the land for development, Cal goes into possession and pays rent yearly.

3. Last year Michael inherited a flat in London with 65 years of the lease unexpired. As Michael already had a house of his own in London, he decided to have the flat sold and he left the flat empty pending sale. Subsequently the landlords, Limetree Properties Ltd, sent a s146 notice to the flat stating that the tenant was in breach of (a) the covenant to keep the windows clean, (b) the covenant to repaint the front door and the window frames before 1 January 1992 and (c) the covenant not to place a window box on the window sill. Michael never saw the notice and two weeks later the landlords peaceably re-entered the flat and changed the locks.

   Advise Michael.

4. In 1980 Peter granted a lease of a house to Thomas for a term of 30 years subject to covenants to pay rent, to keep the house in a good state of repair and not to use the house for business purposes. Performance of the tenant's covenants was guaranteed by a surety, Simon. In 1989 Thomas granted a sublease of the house to Richard for a term of ten years and in

1990 Thomas assigned his lease to Stephen. In 1991 Peter assigned his reversion to Arthur.

Arthur has received no rent this year, the house is in urgent need of repair and Richard is proposing to start a business in the house.

What remedies does Arthur have, and against whom?

5. a) 'An agreement for a lease is as good as a lease'.

    Discuss.

    and

    b) In 1993, the Fee Simple owner of Redacre (an unregistered property) gave a written seven year lease to T at a rental of £10,000 per year payable quarterly. T went into possession and paid rent to L on a monthly basis. Recently L sold Redacre to P who now wishes to obtain possession of Redacre on the grounds that T has broken a repairing covenant.

    Advise P.

Further Reading

- HLT Textbook Chapter 10
- Gray Chapter 17, pp673–765, Chapter 18, pp777–868 and Chapter 19
- Bridge 'Tenancies at Will in the Court of Appeal: *Javad* v *Aqil*' [1991] CLJ 232
- Bridge 'All's Well that Ends Well? Certainty of Leasehold Terms' [1993] CLJ 26
- Bridge 'First Tenant's Liability in the Lords: Assignment of Leave by Original Tenant: Continuing Obligations' [1994] CLJ 28
- Bridge 'Former Tenants, Future Liabilities and the Privity of Contract Principle: The Landlord and Tenant (Covenants) Act 1995' [1996] CLJ 313
- Bridge 'Keeping the Customer Occupied? The Business of Sub-letting' [1996] CLJ 197
- Davey 'Privity of Contract and Leases – Reform at Last' (1996) 59 MLR 78

- Gravells 'Forfeiture of Leases and Mortgages' (1994) 110 LQR 15
- Hopkins 'Leasehold Reform' (1995) 58 MLR 547
- Sparkes 'Certainty of Leasehold Terms' (1993) 109 LQR 93
- Tee 'Mrs Doubtfire's Doubtful Notice' [1994] CLJ 227
- Wilde 'Certainty of Leasehold Terms' (1994) 57 MLR 117

TOPIC 7:   Licences

1. As an interest in land

a) Types

Whether or not a licence is revocable or binds a third party depends upon which type of licence has been created. There are four categories:

- Bare licences

- Licences coupled with an interest (a profit à prendre)

- Contractual licences

- Licences protected in equity or by estoppel

b) Revocability

- Bare licence: revocable by licensor at any time provided that he gives the licensee reasonable notice

- Licence coupled with an interest: irrevocable

- Contractual licences: licensor has no right to eject a licensee in breach of contract even if licence is not specifically enforceable. The revocability of *commercial* contractual licences depends on the terms of the licence, express or implied. A contractual licence may also arise form a *domestic* relationship eg persons occupying land under an informal family arrangement that has broken down, and the court will decide upon the terms according to what reason and justice require, eg a term that the licence shall not be revoked until the children of the household are past school age.

- Licences protected in equity or by estoppel: usually the equitable device employed to create the interest in the land will ensure that the licence is irrevocable, whether it is a full fee simple, a tenancy or a licence under a constructive trust.

Key cases

- *Hurst v Picture Theatres Ltd* [1915] 1 KB 1

- *Ives* v *High* [1967] 2 QB 379

- *Verrall* v *Great Yarmouth Borough Council* [1980] 1 All ER 839

- *Winter Garden Theatres* v *Millennium Products* [1948] AC 173

- *Wood* v *Leadbitter* (1845) 13 M and W 838

c) Effect on third parties

- Bare licence: not binding on third parties

- Licences coupled with an interest: binding on third parties

- Contractual licences: not binding on third parties, even successors in title with notice of the licence, but note that estoppel may create a binding effect – see much criticised decision in *Errington* v *Errington and Woods* [1952] 1 KB 290. The solution of the constructive trust might also be developed so as to bind third parties even where the original licence was purely contratual (see (d) below).

- Licences protected by estoppel or in equity: binding on third parties. The constructive trust device has sometimes been used to bind purchasers with notice of the licence: *Binions* v *Evans* [1972] Ch 359. Equity will also enforce a licence against successors in title with notice where the original licence conferred a *benefit* on the licensor which the successors in title is enjoying, ie licensor must accept the *burdens* imposed by the licence in order to enjoy the benefit: see *Ives* v *High* [1967] 2 QB 379.

Key cases

- *Binion* v *Evans*, above

- *Chandler* v *Kerley* [1978] 1 WLR 693

- *Crabb* v *Arun DC* [1976] Ch 179

- *DHN Food Distributors* v *LB Tower Hamlets* [1976] 3 All ER 462

- *Dilwyn* v *Llewellyn* (1862) 4 De GF and J 517
- *Errington* v *Errington and Woods*, above
- *Inwards* v *Baker* [1965] 2 QB 29
- *Ives* v *High*, above
- *Pascoe* v *Turner* [1979] 1 WLR 431

2. The lease/licence distinction

a) The modern test?

Exclusive possession is an essential feature of a lease, so (*Street* v *Mountford* [1985] 2 WLR 877) if exclusive possession is not granted, the agreement can only be a licence. However, it is possible for the grantee to be given exclusive possession and still not have a lease. Whether an agreement is a lease or a licence depends on the true intention of the parties. Tests used by the courts in determining the intention to create a licence include:

- The words used: this is evidence of the parties' intention but not conclusive.

- Concurrent rights of possession: where the landlord reserves concurrent rights of possession there is only a licence but the reservation of a right of access for specific purposes does not prevent the grant of a lease.

- Family arrangements and similar arrangements: usually regarded as licences, there being no intention to create a formal landlord-tenant relationship.

- Employees: (eg caretakers, house surgeons) who are required to reside in premises as a necessary part of their duties are licensees.

- Mistresses: where a mistress occupies premises provided by her lover, the courts have tended to regard her as a licensee.

- Circumstances: the court will look at the circumstances in which the agreement was reached, and this is the ultimate test.

Key case

- *Street* v *Mountford* [1985] 2 WLR 877

b) Certainty of term

Types of tenancy – terms certain; yearly tenancies; periodic tenancies; tenancies at will

Key cases

- *Lace* v *Chantler* [1944] KB 368

- *Prudential Assurance Co Ltd* v *London Residuary Body* [1992] 3 WLR 279

c) Rent

The need for rent was challenged by Fox LJ in *Ashburn Anstalt* v *Arnold* [1988] 2 All ER 147 on the basis that the need for rent was negatived by the definition of 'term of years absolute' in s205(1)(xxvii) LPA 1925 as ' ... a term of years (taking effect either in possession or in reversion whether or nor at a rent)'. It is likely that this argument is not affected by the overruling of *Ashburn Anstalt* v *Arnold* by the House of Lords in *Prudential Assurance Co Ltd* v *London Residuary Body* [1992] 3 WLR 279.

Key cases

- *Ashburn Anstalt* v *Arnold*, above

- *Prudential Assurance Co Ltd* v *London Residuary Body*, above

Statute

- Law of Property Act 1925, s205

d) Exclusive possession

As noted above, exclusive possession is crucial in establishing the evidence of a tenancy and the absence of a licence.

However, the question of exclusive possession may continue to create problems when trying to establish whether an occupier is a tenant or a lodger. If an occupier does not have exclusive possession but the landlord provides no services, the courts may well have difficulty in applying Lord Templeman's test from *Street* v *Mountford*.

In *Hadjiloucas* v *Crean* [1987] 3 All ER 1008, the Court of Appeal concluded that Lord Templeman's test may be too wide to cover some non-exclusive possession agreements, and do not necessarily cover certain examples of multiple occupation. Depending on the facts, it could be that:

- Each occupier is a licensee if he cannot exclude others; or

- There are parallel leases where each tenant has a right to exclude all others; or

- The agreement produces a joint tenancy with a collective form of exclusive possession in all the co-owners.

See further the House of Lords approach in *AG Securities* v *Vaughan: Antoniades* v *Villiers* [1988] 3 WLR 1205.

Key cases

- *AG Securities* v *Vaughan; Antoniades* v *Villiers* [1988] 3 WLR 1205

- *Aslan* v *Murphy* [1989] 3 All ER 130

- *Westminster CC* v *Clarke* [1992] 2 WLR 229

- *Hadjiloucas* v *Crean*, above

Statutes

- Rent Act 1977

- Housing Act 1988

Sample Question

'A disposition or licence properly passeth no interest nor alters or transfers property in anything ...' (Vaughan CJ).

'The doctrine of the licence ... is no more than a mechanism by which the law sanctions the informal creation of proprietary rights in land.' (Moriarty).

Does either of these statements accurately reflect the current status of licences in property law?

Further Reading

- HLT Textbook Chapter 10 section 10.5 and Chapter 13
- Gray Chapters 13, 15 and 19
- Cooke 'Reliance and Estoppel' (1995) 111 LQR 389
- Kerbel 'The Licensee's Period of Grace' [1996] CLJ 229
- Milne 'Proprietary Estoppel in a Procrustean Bed' (1995) 58 MLR 412
- Townend 'Continuing Difficulties in Distinguishing the Lease from the Licence: Recent Cases' (1995) 29 LTeach 352

TOPIC 8:   Covenants

1. Covenants between freeholders: definitions

a) A covenant is a promise contained in a deed. The deed is usually a conveyance of a freehold estate in land, but the covenant may be contained in a separate deed. The type of promise in such deeds usually concerns the land, for example:

- a promise not to build a factory

- a promise to maintain a fence

- a promise to keep land as open space

But the parties can make any type of promise, although enforceability promises not concerning the land is limited. The person who makes the promise is the 'covenantor'. The person to whom it is made is the 'covenantee'.

b) The land owned by the covenantee has the benefit of the covenant, and so is the 'dominant tenement'. The land owned by the covenantor has the burden of the covenant and is the 'servient tenement'. This is illustrated by the following diagram where X originally owned the whole of Greenacre and sold part to Y, taking from Y a covenant not to use the land for business purposes.

X
(Original owner of Greenacre)

	Greenacre	
	Green 1/2 acre	Green - other 1/2 acre
Benefit	X	Y
	Covenantee	Covenantor – not to use for business purposes

X	Y
Covenantee Receives the benefit	Covenantor Makes the covenant and becomes subject to the burden
Dominant land	Servient land

Benefit

Burden

Benefit
Is the covenant enforceable by persons who subsequently acquire X's land – Green 1/2 acre?

Burden
Can the covenant bind persons who subsequently acquire Y's land – Green – other 1/2 acre – so that later successors in the title of covenantor can be sued on the covenant?

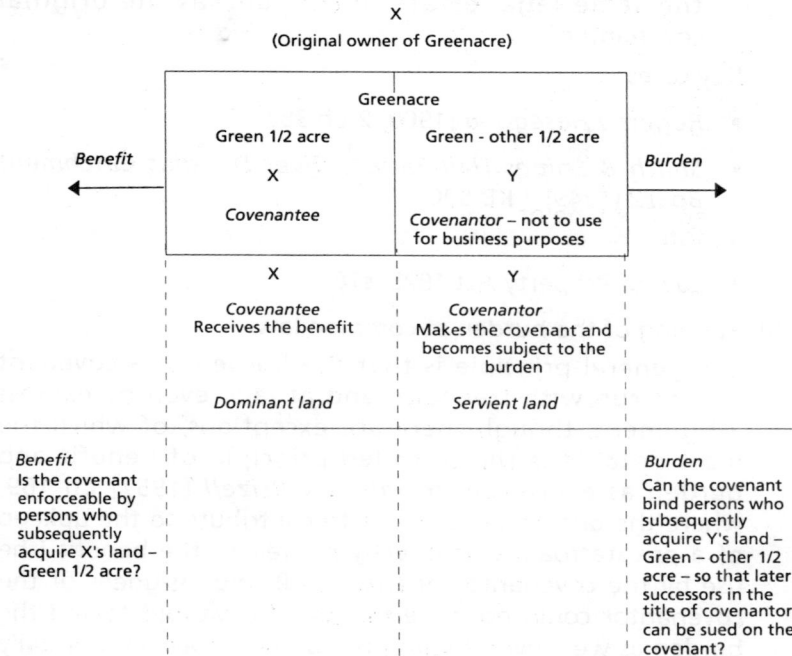

2. Restrictive covenants

a) Running of the benefit at common law

The benefit of a covenant runs with the land of the covenantee at common law, without express assignment, provided that four conditions are satisfied:

- The covenant touches and concerns the land of the covenantee;

- There is an intention that the benefit should run with land owned by the covenantee at the date of the covenant;

- The covenantee must have the legal estate in the land which is to be benefited at the time of making the covenant; and

- An assignee seeking to enforce the covenant must have

the same legal estate in the land as the original covenantee.

Key cases

- *Rogers* v *Hosegood* [1900] 2 Ch 388

- *Smith & Snipes Hall Farm* v *River Douglas Catchment Board* [1949] 2 KB 500

Statute

- Law of Property Act 1925, s78

b) Running of the burden at common law

The general principle is that the burden of a covenant cannot run with freehold land at law, even by express assignment, though there are exceptions, of which the most notable is the so-called principle of benefit and burden as expressed in *Halsall* v *Brizell* [1957] Ch 169, where the burden (a covenant to contribute to the upkeep of a private road) was directly related to the benefit (the use by the covenantor of that road), the assignees of the covenantor could not take the benefit without taking the burden as well, even though the burden does not normally run at law.

Key case

- *Halsall* v *Brizell*, above

c) Running of the benefit in equity

A successor in title of the original covenantee will have the benefit of a covenant in equity provided that four conditions are satisfied:

- The covenant is negative in substance. The test is whether compliance will require the expenditure of money by the covenantor, or some other active step.

- The covenant touches and concerns the land of the covenantee.

- The covenantee has retained land capable of benefiting from the covenant and the covenant was made for the benefit of that land. A landlord's reversion is a sufficient interest in land to allow him to enforce restrictive covenants in the head lease against subtenants.

It is a question of fact whether this requirement is made out, but some degree of physical proximity between the dominant and servient tenements is required.

- The benefit of the covenant has passed to the covenantee.

The benefit may pass by annexation, assignment or through building schemes.

- Annexation
  Key cases

  - *Re Ballard's Conveyance* [1937] Ch 473

  - *Rogers* v *Hosegood*, above

- Assignment
  Key case

  - *Newton Abbot Co-op Society Ltd* v *Williamson & Treadgold* [1952] Ch 286

- Building schemes
  Key cases

  - *Baxter* v *Four Oaks Properties* [1965] Ch 816

  - *Brunner* v *Greenslade* [1971] Ch 993

  - *Re Dolphin's Conveyance* [1970] 1 Ch 654

  - *Elliston* v *Reacher* [1908] 2 Ch 374

- Statutory annexation
  Key cases

  - *Federated Homes* v *Millodge Properties* [1980] 1 WLR 594

  - *Roake* v *Chadha* [1983] 3 All ER 503

  Statute

  - Law of Property Act 1925, s78

d) Running of the burden in equity

A successor in title of the original covenantor will be subject to the burden of the covenant in equity provided that four conditions are satisfied:

- The covenant is negative in substance
- The covenant was made for the benefit of land retained by the covenantee
- The covenant must touch and concern the dominant land
- The burden of the covenant was intended to run with the land of the covenantor

Key cases

- *Haywood* v *Brunswick Permanent Benefit BS* (1881) 8 QBD 403
- *Smith & Snipes Hall Farm* v *River Douglas Catchment Board* [1949] 2 KB 500
- *Tulk* v *Moxhay* (1848) 2 Ph 774

Statute

- Law of Property Act 1925, s79

Running of covenants

	Benefit	Burden
Common law	Yes ────────▶	No
Equity	(Yes)	Yes Provided that the covenant is negative/ restrictive

NB: Burden of a positive covenant does not run – neither at common law nor in equity

e) Discharge/modification

In general a restrictive covenant remains enforceable indefinitely, but there are various methods by which one may be discharged:

- The person entitled to the benefit expressly releases it (ie waives his right to enforce it) by acquiescing to the breach.

- The person entitled to the benefit impliedly releases it by acting in such a way that it would be inequitable to enforce the covenant.

- It may be discharged or modified by the Lands Tribunal on application made under s84 LPA 1925 as amended by s28 LPA 1969. The Lands Tribunal may award compensation or impose an alternative restrictive covenant.

The grounds for application are:

- The person entitled to the benefit (being of full age and capacity) has expressly or impliedly consented.

- The proposed discharge will not injuriously affect the person entitled to the benefit.

- The restrictions are obsolete due to changes in the neighbourhood (this will not be so if the restriction is of real value, or the value of property is affected).

- The restrictions are of no substantial advantage or value.

- The restrictions are contrary to the public interest.

Statute

- Law of Property Act 1925, s84

Sample Questions

1. In 1873, the Earl of Midshire divided an estate into thirty five lots. He sold each plot to individual purchasers imposing restrictive covenants (inter alia) prohibiting the building of more than one residential unit on each plot.

In 1991, Arabella purchased one of the plots and obtained planning permission to build a row of six terraced cottages on the land.

Balvinder owns the freehold of an adjoining plot and wishes to enforce the restrictive covenant against Arabella.

Advise Balvinder as to his chances of success.

2. In 1965 Fred purchased two adjoining plots of land. In 1966 he built a house on the first plot and he sold the other plot to Georgina. In 1967 Georgina built a house on her plot. In 1991 Fred sold his house to Ellen.

Georgina has now sought your advice over the following matters:

a) Ellen intends to build a large conservatory on the rear of her house, which Georgina fears will interfere with the view from the rear of Georgina's house and will considerably darken it;

b) The construction of the conservatory will involve the destruction of a drain running from Georgina's property across Ellen's property. The drain allows rainfall to drain away from Georgina's land and without it Georgina fears her land will become flooded;

c) Fred allowed Georgina to store coal in an old shed on his land. Ellen has now told Georgina she may no longer store anything there and that she must remove any of her property in the shed immediately.

Advise Georgina.

3. Alan owned Blackacre and the adjoining Whiteacre, and in 1960 he sold Blackacre to Douglas who covenanted with Alan and his successors-in-title (a) not to let the property fall into disrepair and (b) not to use the property for business purposes.

On the assumption that the land is unregistered, consider how far these covenants will be enforceable:

a) by a lessee of Whiteacre against Douglas;

b) by Alan against an adverse possessor of Blackacre; and

c) by a purchaser of Whiteacre against a purchaser of Blackacre.

Further Reading

- HLT Textbook Chapter 11
- Gray Chapter 22
- Gardner 'Two Maxims of Equity' [1995] CLJ 63
- Gravells 'Enforcement of Positive Covenants Affecting Freehold Land' (1994) 110 LQR 346
- Ockleton 'A Roof too Far' [1994] CLJ 446

TOPIC 9:   Easements

1. Characteristics

There are four essentials:

- There must be a dominant and a servient tenement.

- The easement must accommodate the dominant tenement.

- The dominant and servient owners must be different persons.

- The right must be capable of forming the subject matter of a grant.

Key cases

- *A-G for Southern Nigeria* v *John Holt* [1915] AC 599

- *Copeland* v *Greenhalf* [1952] Ch 488

- *Re Ellenborough Park* [1956] Ch 131

- *Grigsby* v *Melville* [1974] 1 WLR 80

- *Hill* v *Tupper* (1863) 2 H and C 121

- *Moody* v *Steggles* (1879) 12 Ch D 261

- *Newman* v *Jones* (1982) unreported

- *Wright* v *Macadam* [1949] 2 KB 744

2. Acquisition

An easement can only be a legal interest in land if it is held for an interest equivalent to a fee simple absolute in possession or a term of years absolute and if it is created by statute, deed or prescription. Any other easement is equitable.

a) Express grant or reservation by servient owner to dominant owner

b) Implied grant

- Easement of necessity: one without which the property retained cannot be used at all, and not one merely necessary to the reasonable enjoyment of the property.

- Intended easements: one necessary to carry out the clear common intention of the parties; eg, the grant of one of a pair of semi-detached houses, the other being retained, implies the mutual grant and reservation of easements of support.

- Easement within the rule in *Wheeldon v Burrows* (1879) 12 Ch D 31: upon the grant of part of a tenement there pass to the grantee as easements all quasi-easements over the land retained which:

  - were continuous and apparent; or

  - were necessary to the reasonable enjoyment of the land granted; and

  - had been, and were at the time of the grant, used by the grantor for the benefit of the part granted.

  The doctrine of *Wheeldon v Burrows* can apply where the common owner sells the quasi dominant land to one person and the quasi servient land to another, provided the sales are contemporaneous.

Key cases

- *Nickerson* v *Barraclough* [1981] 2 All ER 369 CA

- *Wong* v *Beaumont Properties* [1965] 1 QB 173

- *Wheeldon* v *Burrows*, above

- *Wheeler and Another* v *JJ Saunders Ltd and Others* [1995] 2 All ER 697

c) Law of Property Act 1925, s62

- By this section, unless a contrary intention is expressed, every conveyance of land passes with it (inter alia) all liberties, privileges, easements, rights and advantages whatsoever, appertaining or reputed to appertain to the land, or any part or, at the time of conveyance, enjoyed with the land or any part. For example, if a landlord renews a lease, having previously allowed the tenant to enjoy certain additional privileges, unless they are expressly excluded, the grant of the new lease converts them into easements enjoyed as of right (provided they are capable of being easements).

- This section only applies to conveyances, not contracts, nor agreements for leases.

Key cases

- *Goldberg* v *Edwards* [1950] Ch 247

- *Long* v *Gowlett* [1923] 2 Ch 177

d) Prescription

Easement acquired by prescription: if long user as of right is proved, the court will presume that the user began lawfully, ie as a result of a grant. There are three methods of prescription (prescription at common law, by lost modern grant and under the Prescription Act 1832), which all rely on proof of continuous user 'as of right':

- Nec vi: no force must be used in order to enjoy the claimed right, nor must user take place under protest from the servient owner.

- Nec clam: if the user is secret the servient owner has no chance to protest, and the user is not as of right. However, the servient owner cannot say that the user was secret if he would have discovered it by reasonable inspection.

- Nec precario: user enjoyed by permission cannot be as of right, even if there is no written contract or periodical payment. Periodical payment shows that the permission was renewed regularly, however, user after permission has lapsed may become user as of right if there is a change in circumstances from which revocation may fairly be implied.

Under the Prescription Act 1832 rights to light and easements other than light are treated differently.

- Easements other than light s2 Prescription Act 1832: as well as user as of right, the claimant must show:

  - use without interruption: s4 Prescription Act 1832

- use for the full period of 20 years (some deductions are possible)

Easements of light: s3 Prescription Act 1832: the actual enjoyment of the access of light to a building for 20 years without interruption makes the right indefeasible unless enjoyed by written consent or agreement. There are different requirements for easements of light:

- User need not be of right, provided that it is not enjoyed by written permission.

- An easement of light can be acquired by a tenant against his landlord.

- There is only one period – 20 years.

- There are no deductions.

- There is no presumption of a grant, and so it may be acquired against an owner who is not a capable grantee.

- Interruptions: 'interruption' has the same meaning as for other easements: see s4 Prescription Act 1832. Any interruption should be a physical obstruction of the light by means of a screen or similar erection. But, under the Rights of Light Act 1959, the interruption can be purely nominal, by registering a light obstruction notice as a local land charge.

Key cases

- *Dalton v Angus* (1881) 6 App Cas 740

- *Mills v Silver* [1991] 2 WLR 324

- *Tehidy Minerals v Norman* [1971] 2 QB 528

Statute

- Prescription Act 1832, s2, s3, s4

Methods of Acquisition of Easements

Easement

Statute — Grant

Express grant — Implied grant — Presumed grant

Easement of necessity or intended easement

Wheeldon v Burrows (1879)12 Ch D 31

s62 LPA 1925

Common law prescription — Lost modern grant — Prescription Act 1832

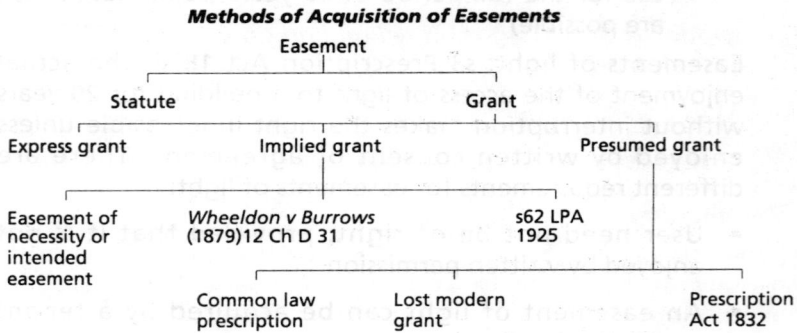

3. Extent of easements

a) A general right of way is not limited to the user contemplated when the grant was made, eg an increase in the number of caravans using a site does not create an excessive user of a right of crossing in order to obtain access to the site which had been acquired by prescription.

b) If a user is a right of way, the intensification or change of user can have dramatic effect on the quality of life of the servient owner. An express grant of a right of way 'at all times and for all purposes' can accommodate intensification and changes in user.

c) However, with an easement of necessity the extent of the implied right is strictly limited and may only be used to maintain the 'mode of enjoyment' of the surrounding, servient, land at the time of the grant.

d) The fact that some land or another part of the building is added to the original dominant tenement will not necessarily destroy a right of way which was previously only appurtenant to the original dominant tenement, but an interference would be actionable if it were substantial; it would not be substantial if it did not interfere with the reasonable use of the right of way: *Celsteel Ltd v Alton House Holdings Ltd* [1985] 1 WLR 204.

Key cases

- *London & Suburban Land & Building Co* v *Carey* (1991) 62 P and CR 480

- *Mills* v *Silver*, above

- *Celsteel* v *Alton House Holdings*, above

4. Termination

There is no statutory procedure to discharge or modify easements as there is for restrictive covenants. There are four methods of extinguishing easements:

- By statute: Commons Registration Act 1965

- By express release

- By implied release

- By unity of ownership and possession

(Note there must be an actual intention to abandon the right; non-user by itself is not enough: *Benn* v *Hardinge* (1992) The Times 13 October.)

Key case

- *Benn* v *Hardinge*, above

Sample Questions

1. 'The importance of the rules relating to the acquisition of easements by implied grant has been considerably reduced by the operation of LPA s62.'

   Discuss.

2. Pat was the owner of Blackacre and Whiteacre, two adjoining pieces of land. In 1978 Pat leased Blackacre to his friend Mick for 10 years at a rent for the purpose of growing vegetables and Pat covenanted to keep the fence which separated the two properties in a good state of repair. In 1980 Mick asked Pat if he could store his tools in a shed on Whiteacre and Pat agreed. In 1982 Mick asked Pat if he and his friends could play football on Whiteacre on Sundays and Pat agreed. In 1988 Pat granted Mick a further 10-year term of Blackacre at a rent. In 1990 Pat died, leaving his entire estate to Rob. Rob has now

refused to allow Mick to store his tools or to play football on Whiteacre, and Rob has also refused to repair the boundary fence.

Advise Mick.

3. Alf and Bert own adjoining farms and from January 1972 Alf has used a rough track leading from his farm over Bert's land to the public road. The surface of the track made it only suitable for use by farm vehicles and when the weather was bad, the track was hardly passable at all. Alf and Bert were friends, and Bert never objected to Alf's use of the track. However, in 1990 Alf and Bert quarrelled and when, in April 1991, Alf began work paving the track with a view to making it suitable for passage by all kinds of vehicles, Bert wrote to Alf withdrawing 'the permission I gave you to use the track' and erected a fence barring access to the track from Alf's farm.

Advise Alf.

Further Reading

- HLT Textbook Chapter 12
- Gray Chapter 21
- Harpum 'The Acquisition of Easements' [1992] CLJ 220

TOPIC 10: Mortgages

1. Types and creation

a) By s85 LPA 1925 a mortgage made after 1925 can be made in one of two ways:

- By demise for a term of years absolute.

- By charge of deed expressed to be by way of legal mortgage: s87 LPA 1925.

b) A legal mortgage can only be created by deed, and can only be created in respect of a legal estate.

c) An equitable mortgage, which may be of either the legal estate or an equitable interest, can be created in one of the following ways:

- A mortgage of an equitable interest: made by conveyance of the whole equitable interest with a proviso for reconveyance on redemption.

- A mortgage of a legal estate not made by deed but by a contract in writing and signed by or on behalf of both parties to the mortgage. Equity treats it as an actual mortgage, provided that the money has actually been advanced.

    The three methods of creating an equitable mortgage of the legal estate are:

    - Depositing with the lender the title deeds to the legal estate as security for the loan (and not for any other purpose). The deposit of title deeds must now be accompanied by some agreement made in writing setting out the mortgage terms signed by or on behalf of both parties.

    - By express agreement made in writing: this must satisfy s2 Law of Property (Miscellaneous Provisions) Act 1989.

    - By equitable charge: this is creating a charge on the land (which is *not* within s87 LPA 1925) without any agreement to make a legal mortgage and without a deposit of title deeds.

Key Case

- *United Bank of Kuwait* v *Sahib* [1996] 3 All ER 215 (CA)

Statute

- Law of Property Act 1925, s85

2. Mortgagor's rights

a) Right to redeem

The right to redeem is the mortgagor's right to pay off all the capital and interest owing under the mortgage and take his land free from the mortgagee's rights. There are two distinct rights to redeem.

- The legal right to redeem is the contractual right at law to redeem on the precise day fixed by the mortgage.

- The equitable right to redeem is the right conferred by equity to redeem at any time after the legal date of redemption has passed on reasonable terms.

b) Equity of Redemption

The equitable right to redeem is not the same as the equity of redemption. The 'equity of redemption' is the total of the mortgagor's rights in the property given by equity, which arise as soon as the mortgage is made. The equity of redemption is an interest in land which can be dealt with just like any other interest in land. The two may be demonstrated in the diagram below.

Key cases

- *Biggs* v *Hodinott* [1898] 2 Ch 307

- *Fairclough* v *Swan Brewery* [1912] AC 565

- *Knightsbridge Estates* v *Byrne* [1939] Ch 441

- *Kreglinger* v *New Patagonia Meat & Cold Storage Co* [1914] AC 25

- *Multi-Service Bookbinding* v *Marden* [1978] 2 WLR 535

- *Noakes* v *Rice* [1902] AC 24

- *Samuel* v *Jarrah Timber* [1904] AC 323
- *Santley* v *Wilde* [1899] 2 Ch 474

Legal or contractual date of redemption

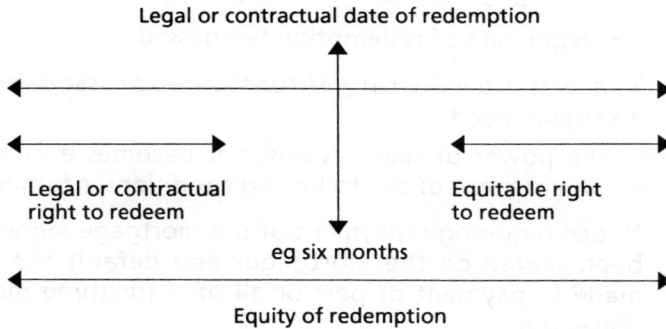

Legal or contractual right to redeem

Equitable right to redeem

eg six months

Equity of redemption

3. Mortgagee's rights

a) Foreclosure

A very severe remedy, foreclosure is the process whereby a court declares that the mortgagor's equitable right to redeem is extinguished, leaving the mortgagee as the legal and equitable owner of the property.

- The legal date of redemption must have passed.

- There must be a court order.

In general the court is reluctant to order foreclosure, especially if the value of the property is greater than the amount owing, and may instead order a sale at the request of any person interested.

Statutes

- Law of Property Act 1925, s91

- Administration of Justice Act 1970, s36

- Administration of Justice Act 1973, s8

b) Sale

The most common remedy, the power of sale enables a mortgagee to recover his capital speedily, and is usually combined with an action to obtain vacant possession to allow the best price to be obtained. The power of sale arises when:

- The mortgage has been made by deed.

- The legal date of redemption has passed.

- There is no contrary intention expressed in the mortgage deed.

Once the power of sale has arisen it becomes exercisable when one or more of the following conditions is fulfilled:

- Notice requiring repayment of the mortgage money has been served on the mortgagor and default has been made in payment of part or all of it for three months thereafter.

- Some interest under the mortgage is two months or more in arrears.

- There has been a breach of some provision (other than the payment covenant) contained in the LPA 1925 or the mortgage deed which should have been observed/ performed by the mortgagor or by someone who concurred in making the mortgage.

No court order is required. The mortgagee is not a trustee of the power of sale, and may sell by any method, but must act in good faith and take reasonable care. The non-building society mortgagee must obtain the true market value of the property.

Key cases

- *Cuckmere Brick* v *Mutual Finance Ltd* [1971] Ch 949

- *Standard Chartered Bank* v *Walker* [1982] 3 All ER 938

Statutes

- Law of Property Act 1925, s101, s103

c) Possession

The mortgagee has a right to possession as soon as the mortgage is executed: s95(4) LPA 1925. If the mortgage is by demise, the mortgagee is a tenant and therefore entitled to possession as against the mortgagor, while a mortgagee whose mortgage is by legal charge has the same rights by statute.

There is nothing inconsistent about granting a mortgagee a possession order, suspended subject to conditions as to payment being met by the mortgagors, and a concurrent money judgment for the entire mortgage debt, suspended for as long as the possession order remains suspended.

Even though the mortgagee has a right of possession he must obtain a court order before he can take possession.

When the mortgaged property includes a dwelling house the court has a discretion by s36 Administration of Justice Act 1970 (as amended) to adjourn the proceedings or to grant a stay of execution where it appears likely to the court that the mortgagor is likely within a reasonable time bring payments up to date. What constitutes a 'reasonable period' was considered in *Cheltenham & Gloucester Building Society* v *Norgan* [1996] 1 All ER 449; [1996] 1 WLR 343 (CA), a landmark ruling which formalises the process of capitalisation where the arrears are added to the original loan.

The court identified a number of considerations likely to be relevant , including:

- How much could the borrower reasonably afford to pay both now and in the future?

- If the borrower had a short term problem in meeting his mortgage commitments, how long was the difficulty likely to last?

- Why had the arrears accumulated?

- How much remained of the original term? and

- Were there any reasons affecting the security which should influence the length of the period for payment?

Note also the possible effect of undue influcence in this area: *Barclays Bank plc* v *O'Brien* [1993] 3 WLR 786 HL (bank's action for possession defeated because it had constructive notice of husband's misrepresentation to wife when persuading her to sign legal charge). See also *Credit Lyonnais Bank Nederland NV* v *Burch* (1996) The Times 1 July (CA).

Key cases

- *Four Maids* v *Dudley Marshall* [1957] Ch 317
- *Quennell* v *Maltby* [1979] 1 WLR 318
- *White* v *City of London Brewery* (1889) 42 Ch D 237
- *Barclays Bank plc* v *O'Brien and Another* [1993] 3 WLR 786
- *Credit Lyonnais Bank Nederland NV* v *Burch* (1996) The Times 1 July (CA)
- *Massey* v *Midland Bank plc* [1995] 1 All ER 929
- *Cheltenham and Gloucester Building Society* v *Norgan* [1996] 1 All ER 449; [1996] 1 WLR 343 (CA): see further Morgan's article, below
- *CIBC Mortgages plc* v *Pitt* [1993] 3 WLR 802
- *National and Provincial Building Society* v *Lloyd* [1996] 1 All ER 630 (CA)
- *Bristol and West Building Society* v *Ellis* (1996) The Times 2 May (CA)

Statutes

- Administration of Justice Act 1970, s36
- Administration of Justice Act 1973, s8

d) Receivership

Receivership achieves much the same result as taking possession without the responsibilities. A statutory power given by s101 LPA 1925, it arises and becomes exercisable under the same circumstances as the power of sale (see above).

- No requirement for a court order.
- The receiver is deemed to be the agent of the mortgagor: s109(2).

Statute

- Law of Property Act 1925, s109

e) The right to tack further advances

The right to tack, is the right of a mortgagee under certain circumstances to add a subsequent loan to an existing loan on the same property mortgaged by the same mortgagor and so to gain priority for this subsequent loan over any intermediate loans by other mortgagees.

Tacking can be if demonstrated by a linear diagram:

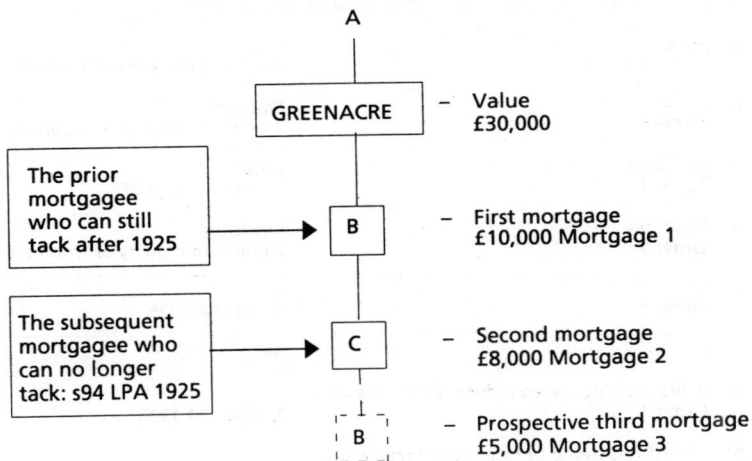

A
|

| GREENACRE | — Value £30,000 |

The prior mortgagee who can still tack after 1925 → B — First mortgage £10,000 Mortgage 1

The subsequent mortgagee who can no longer tack: s94 LPA 1925 → C — Second mortgage £8,000 Mortgage 2

B — Prospective third mortgage £5,000 Mortgage 3

If A now wishes to borrow a further £5,000 on the security of Greenacre and B is prepared to lend the £5,000, he will wish to know whether he can 'tack' mortgage 3 to mortgage 1 in order to obtain priority for his combined loan of £15,000 before C.

Section 94 LPA 1925 provides that the two loans may be tacked if one of three conditions is satisfied:

- B has arranged with C to enable mortgage 1 and mortgage 3 to be added together.

- There is an obligation in mortgage 1 to make further advances.

- B has no notice of mortgage 2 created with C.

4. Priority of Mortgages: unregistered land

The priority of mortgages of unregistered land is summed up by the following table. 'R' stands for registrable, 'NR' for non-registrable:

First	Order of creation	Second
1.		**NR**
Priority depends on whether mortgages are legal or equitable.		
a) Legal Order 1		Legal 2 unless first guilty of fraud etc
b) Legal Order 1		Equitable 2 unless first guilty of fraud etc
c) Equitable Order 1		Legal 2 unless second BFP
d) Equitable Order 1		Equitable 2 unless first guilty of fraud etc
2. NR Order 1		**R** 2: s13 LPA 1925
3. R		**NR**
a) If first not registered before second created Order 1		2: s198 LPA 1925
b) If first registered before second created Order 2		1: s4 LCA 1972
4. R		**R**
a) If first registered before second created Order 1		2: s198 LPA 1925
b) If second created and registered before first registered Order 2		1: s4 LCA 1972

c) If both created before first registered, second registered after first, conflict
   Order 1
   Order 2
		2: s97 LPA 1925
		1: s4 LCA 1972

5. Priority of mortgages: registered land

The rules relating to priority of mortgages are also complex, and depend on the nature of the mortgage.

a) Registered charges rank in the order in which they are entered on the register (cf s97 LPA 1925) and not in the order in which they are created: see s29 LRA 1925 and *Williams & Glyn's Bank* v *Boland* [1981] AC 487.

b) Other mortgages: the position of mortgages not protected by registration or the former special mortgage caution was considered in *Barclays Bank Ltd* v *Taylor* [1974] Ch 137. An equitable mortgage was created by the deposit with the bank of the land certificate, the bank registering a notice of deposit. The registered proprietors then contracted to sell the property to the Taylors, who entered a caution to protect their estate contract. The Court of Appeal held that the bank's mortgage was effective in equity, and thus took priority to that of the Taylors, who also had only an equitable interest. Such mortgages would appear to rank in priority in order of date of entry of the caution or notice of deposit.

6. Priority of equitable interests

The priority of mortgages of an equitable interest is governed by the rule in *Dearle* v *Hall* (1828) 3 Russ 1, as amended by ss137 and 138 LPA 1925: priority depends upon the order in which the trustees received notice from the mortgagees. The rule applies to both registered and unregistered land.

Sample Questions

1. 'Once a mortgage always a mortgage and nothing but a mortgage. The meaning of that is that the mortgage shall not make any stipulation which will prevent a mortgagor, who has paid principal, interest, and costs, from getting back his mortgaged property in the condition in which he parted with it.' (per Lord Davey)

   Explain this statement and consider the extent to which it remains true today.

2. In 1990 Jack and Jill, husband and wife, purchased the fee simple of 'The Wine Bar' where they have sold drinks and snacks. The title is unregistered and the conveyance was made to Jack alone. The purchase price was £40,000; Jack and Jill each provided £10,000 and the X Wine Co Ltd lent £20,000 on the security of a legal mortgage from Jack. In the mortgage Jack covenanted:

a) that for ten years he would purchase all wines and spirits for 'The Wine Bar' from the X Wine Co Ltd;

b) that the mortgage should be irredeemable for ten years; and

c) that after the expiration of the ten years the X Wine Co Ltd should for a further five years have the right of first refusal at market price, if Jack should decide to sell 'The Wine Bar'.

Profits from the business have been falling and Jack believes this has been caused by the poor quality and selection of the wines supplied by the X Wine Co Ltd.

Advise Jack:

a) whether he is bound by any of the above mentioned covenants;

b) whether, if he falls into arrears with payments of mortgage interest, the X Wine Co Ltd will be able to obtain possession of, and sell, 'The Wine Bar'.

Further Reading

- HLT Textbook Chapter 14
- Cheshire and Burn Chapter 21 p623
- Fehlberg 'The Husband, the Bank, the Wife and her Signature – The Sequel' (1996) 59 MLR 675
- Lawson 'O'Brien and its Legacy: Principle, Equity and Certainty?' [1995] CLJ 280
- Morgan 'Mortgage Arrears and the Family Home' (1996) 112 LQR 553

TOPIC 11: Adverse Possession and Restrictions on Ownership

1. Periods

The main limitation periods for land law purposes are:

- Six years for simple contracts, arrears of rent, tort (s5 Limitation Act (LA) 1980).

- Twelve years from the date on which the right of action accrued for actions on a deed (s15 LA 1980).

- Twelve years for actions for recovery of land or money charged on land (s16 LA 1980).

Statute

- Limitation Act 1980, ss5, 15, 16

2. Discontinuance/dispossession

Time begins to run as soon as:

- The owner has been dispossessed or has discontinued his possession.

- Adverse possession has been taken by some other person. Adverse possession is possession inconsistent with the title of the true owner, and is a matter of fact depending on the circumstances of each case.

Key cases

- *Buckingham CC* v *Moran* [1989] 2 All ER 225

- *Marsden* v *Miller* (1992) The Times 23 January

- *Powell* v *Macfarlane* (1977) 38 P and CR 452

- *Seddon* v *Smith* (1877) 36 LT 168

- *Treloar* v *Nute* [1976] 1 WLR 1295

3. Trusts

a) Adverse possession of trust property does not bar the trustee's title until all the beneficiaries are barred; for example, if land is held on trust for sale for X for life, then to Y for life and then to Z, 12 years' possession by S, a squatter, against X will bar only X; time will not start to run against Y until X's death, and similarly time will not run against Z until Y's death, and S will only bar the trustee's legal estate by 12 years' adverse possession after Y's death.

b) A trustee can never acquire title by limitation against the beneficiaries. Time does not run in favour of a beneficiary against the trustees unless the beneficiary is solely and absolutely entitled. This would occur when a purchaser is let into possession before conveyance: s18 LA 1980.

Statutes

- Limitation Act 1980, s15(6), s18, s21

4. Leases

a) Time does not begin to run against the reversioner if the tenant is dispossessed until the lease expires, because until then he has no right to possession.

b) A tenant cannot acquire title against his landlord during the currency of the lease because his possession is not adverse.

c) Failure to pay the rent only bars the landlord's right to recover any unpaid instalment after six years. The landlord's title will, however, be barred if a third party is in adverse receipt of rent for 12 years. If the rent is 'not less than ten pounds a year' see Sch 1 Pt I para 6 LA 1980.

Key case

- *Fairweather* v *St Marylebone Property Co* [1963] AC 510

5. Effect of lapse of time

Once the limitation period has been achieved:

a) The owner's title is extinguished in that he can no longer take legal proceedings to recover the property: s17 LA 1980.

b) The squatter acquires the title that the person he dispossessed had, subject to all third party rights.

The nature of the squatter's title was described by Lord Radcliffe in *Fairweather v St Marylebone Property Co Ltd* [1963] AC 510:

'He is not at any stage ... a successor to the title of the man he has dispossessed. He comes in and remains in always by right of possession, which in due course becomes incapable of disturbance as time exhausts the one or more periods allowed by statute for successful intervention. His title, therefore, is never derived through but arises always in spite of the dispossessed owner.'

Fairweather was distinguished in *Spectrum Investment Co v Holmes* [1981] 1 WLR 221: in the case of registered land, if the squatter registered his rights under the LRA 1925, once the limitation period has run, those rights could not be defeated by a subsequent surrender of the lease between the original lessee and the landlord. In *Fairweather* the House of Lords did not have to consider the effect of registration of the squatter's title.

c) Leases: unless the landlord has reserved a right of forfeiture for breach of covenant and a covenant is broken he cannot eject a squatter until the lease has expired. If, however, the dispossessed tenant surrenders his lease, the lease merges with the reversion and the landlord can sue immediately for possession. The rule in *Spectrum Investment Co v Holmes*, above, will operate in the same way. The result is the same if the tenant acquires the landlord's reversion.

  • The tenant will continue to remain liable under the covenants in the lease if he was the original tenant, if there is privity of contract, but not if there was only privity of estate.

  • There is no privity of estate between a squatter and the landlord, and so only restrictive covenants are directly enforceable against him. He is, however, liable to distress if the rent is not paid.

  • If he does pay rent he will become a periodic tenant.

Section 75 LRA 1925 provides that the Limitation Act 1980 applies to registered land as it does to unregistered land, with one important distinction: when an interest would have been extinguished in the case of unregistered land then in the case of registered land it will not be extinguished, instead it is deemed to be held in trust by the registered proprietor for the person who has acquired title against him. The effect is that no legal title can vest in the adverse possessor until he has been registered as proprietor. Until then the registered proprietor's estate is held on trust for the adverse possessor.

Key cases

- *Fairweather* v *St Marylebone Co*, above
- *Spectrum Investment Co* v *Homes* [1981] 1 WLR 221

Statute

- Land Registration Act 1925, s75

Sample Questions

1. 'The courts have interpreted the concept of adverse possession so restrictively that a person claiming land by possession is unlikely to be successful except in rare cases.'

   Discuss.

2. Peter owned a house at No 12 Church Street and Quentin owned the neighbouring house at No 14 Church Street. The titles to both properties were registered under the Land Registration Acts. In 1975 Peter erected a tool-shed partly on his own garden and partly on a strip of the garden of No 14 without Quentin's consent. In 1985 Peter sold No 12 to James who continued to use the shed and in 1990 Quentin sold No 14 to Henry. Henry now wants James to remove the shed.

   Advise James. How would your advice differ if the land was unregistered?

Further Reading

- HLT Textbook Chapters 15 and 17
- Cheshire and Burn Chapters 26 and 29 (relevant pages)

TOPIC 12:   Reform: The New Law on Trusts of Land

The Trusts of Land and Appointment of Trustees Act 1996 is effective from 1 January 1997. Part I of the Act affects in particular Topics 3, 4 and 5.

1. Key points

- A new concept, 'the trust of land', is created to replace strict settlements and trusts for sale.

- Generally speaking no new strict settlement can be created under the Settled Land Act.

- All trusts for sale become trusts of land whether created before or after commencement.

- The doctrine of conversion is abolished.

- Trustees are no longer under a duty to sell land. Rather they have a power to sell and a power to retain the land.

- Additional rights for beneficiaries are created.

- Wider powers for the court are provided.

2. Purpose of the reforms

The Act aims to make the law more comprehensible to lay people, it is an amending rather than a consolidating statute.

The Act removes the complication of the pre-Act system of two distinct ways of holding land in trust. It is retrospective except as regard pre-Act strict settlements. Accordingly, the Settled Land Act regime still remains (with some amendments) part of English land law – at least in the short term. However, strict settlements will be phased out. The timescale in this regard is uncertain (for example it will depend upon how frequently on a resettlement of a pre-Act settlement advantage is taken of the facility to convert to a trust of land).

Sample Questions

See Questions in Topics 3, 4 and 5 and advise in the light of the 1996 Act reforms.

Further Reading

- Law Update 1997 Chapter 17 Land Law section on Settlements of Land and Co-Ownership HLT Publications
- Law Commission Report *Transfer of Land: Trusts for Land* no 181 (1989)